BECOMING A FEMALE CEO

LIFE, BUSINESS, AND INTUITION

RENÉ MURATA

CONTENTS

INTRODUCTION

I didn't always see myself as becoming a CEO. In fact, I thought I'd be an artist, or a flight attendant or maybe even a marketing agent of some kind, traveling the world, exploring different cultures, different countries and learning languages, but never a CEO.

Life turned out differently than I expected…waaay differently. However, I believe that may often be the case.

How about you? What plans did you have for yourself? Chances are, what you are doing now is far different than what you envisioned.

Whether or not that's the case, if you are reading this book, then you probably have some thoughts about stepping into leadership or running your own business. So welcome and congratulations! This is quite an undertaking and can, at times, be a bit challenging. However, it can also be very rewarding.

Now, I'm not going to lie to you and say it will be easy. Being in a leadership role does mean work. However, it can be fun, exciting, even exhilarating. In leadership, you have the opportunity to empower those that work with and for you, and you can influence the success (or not) of your team, and by extension, the business, and ultimately create positive experiences for your clients.

My goal with this book is to share with you how I navigated the journey to become a female CEO with the hopes that it will help you with your journey and maybe even provide inspiration for those moments that might feel a little heavier.

I don't know about you, but I didn't have a lot of self-esteem, and I believed that to be a CEO you had to have lots of self-esteem. I also believed that you had to have a vision and desire to manage other people. I didn't. In fact, I didn't really get on well with others. Not that I didn't get along, I just didn't trust others, so I couldn't see myself working well with, for, or "above" anyone.

Life had different plans for me.

By the time I got to college, I had a child and was a single parent. Travel no longer felt possible. Art no longer felt practical.

I started studying languages. I'm not sure what I thought I'd do with them, but I loved them. Then, during a required math course, I met my husband.

From that point forward, everything shifted. I now had a different focus. However, owning a business and being CEO were still not part of my vision, paying the bills and having a steady income was.

During college, I ended up with a B.A. in physics and a B.S. in mathematics (a story all by itself). From there I went to work as an assistant to an electrical engineer who openly claimed to not "play well with others". Two weeks after going to work for him, I was called into a meeting. He wanted me to "translate" for him by way of explaining his thinking on his current project to the computer engineer, mechanical engineer, marketing director and operations manager. Apparently, they were struggling to understand his point of view. I ended up explaining back and forth between the different disciplines. During my two years working for him, I discovered that I was very good at interpreting what others really wanted to say and in turn, explaining those thoughts to others that needed to hear and understand… in other words, facilitation and negotiation.

After two years, my husband and I moved to another state where I went to work in an oil refinery. Over that period, I would be promoted from administrative assistant to engineering assistant, and finally to assistant engineer. I would also learn how difficult it was/is for a non-chemical engineering female to succeed in that industry (or maybe, how difficult it was for a woman to succeed in any industry dominated by men.)

During that time, I had to prove, not only to the men, that I was capable of doing my job, but also to the few women that had "made it'. The women surprised me. I felt like there are so few women at the top, why didn't they help others more?

That question, and the subsequent answer, is what opened my mind to the possibility of leadership. First, though, I had to embark on a journey that would take me down a very different path to the one I started on. I would find myself working in a very male dominated environment while at the same time exploring my spirituality.

What follows is an accounting of what I had to learn, heal, allow, and release while Becoming a CEO.

Really, my journey into leadership began with an understanding that I had to address my biases about leadership in general. In my mind, being a leader meant that I had to lean heavily into a more masculine persona; competitive, aggressive, and domineering. The problem was that I wanted something different. I wanted to bring compassion, empathy, kindness, and empowerment into the workplace.

Have you thought about what type of leader you want to be? Which qualities and attributes do you have and/or want for your leadership role? Kindness? Strength? Empathy? Do you know how to bring forward the traits you want and lead with them?

With no mentors, I wasn't sure how to lead the way I wanted to lead. Everything about leadership, I had learned through observation and doing. One thing I knew is that to be successful, I had to find a way into leadership that allowed me to be ALL of who I am, intelligent, strong, outspoken, empathic, collaborative, and caring.

It is my belief that the more people that lead from a place of authenticity, compassion, service, joy, empowerment, strength, and kindness, the more we will see workplaces shifting from toxic working environments to empowering ones.

Thus, you will find that throughout the book, I will be focusing on what I've found to be three key components of the CEO's journey: releasing core limiting beliefs, embodiment of both our masculine and feminine energies, and understanding and managing team dynamics.

Why these three things vs some of the alternatives?

Because I have found that the most impact in a person's ability to step into CEO ship is in understanding these three areas.

For example, if you have beliefs that you aren't good enough, smart enough, pretty enough, etc., then, no matter what you do, say, think, or practice, you will be exactly what you believe; not good enough, smart enough, pretty enough, etc.

Also, everyone has both masculine and feminine traits. When you lean too heavily on one, you find yourself out of balance. This leads to toxic behaviors. So, acknowledging and embodying ALL of who you are is the surest way to empowered leadership.

And finally, the third area is team dynamics. You have to understand how to manage, inspire, and lead a team in order to grow your business. This includes managing and addressing conflict, delegating, and decision making.

Within each of the sections, you will find stories, from both my journey, and those of some of my clients, that I hope you find encouraging as well as supportive in your journey.

I will be sharing some of the different healing and learning modalities that I have picked up along the way in the hopes that they inspire you. Please understand that for the sake of brevity I am only sharing a few of my favorite modalities and that not every modality is for everyone. Also, I want you to feel free to take them, use them, modify them or discard them as appropriate for you. They are presented for you to use as a jumping off point to explore potentially new ways for you to heal.

EnJoy, Love, and Light,

René

CORE LIMITING BELIEFS

L et's talk about core limiting beliefs; what are they and why is it important to understand and deal with them? As we go through the following pages, I'll share with you how I came to recognize mine, where they came from and how they impacted my leadership and life in the hope that my story may inspire you to recognize yours and help you deal with them.

So, I'm curious, do you know what core limiting beliefs are? Do you know what yours are and how they are impacting you? In case you are like I was, I'll define them here.

Core limiting beliefs are central beliefs that you have about yourself. They live beneath the surface, in your subconscious. For many of us, it is that "am I good enough, smart enough, pretty enough" question that we are constantly asking ourselves. These beliefs might be the thought that you can't do something or that you don't deserve something you want and desire.

They are like an invisible force holding you back from living your best life. You may not realize they are there. Instead, you may feel like the world is conspiring against you. These beliefs often originate from negative things that happened in our childhood and youth. They aren't facts, but rather a viewpoint, or lens through which you see the world.

When you have limiting beliefs like this, they can show up in how you make decisions, how you respond or react to someone, as well as in your overall confidence. Core limiting beliefs can lead you to avoid conflict, or alternatively, you might show up as aggressive in order to "prove" something. Either way, core limiting beliefs have a powerful, and usually subtle negative impact on your life, blocking your road to success.

The thing about core beliefs is that as you journey through life, they may show up at different times, in different ways, and at different levels of understanding. In other words, you may release some belief about not being good enough. Then, later in life, when you've achieved something new, you may find that this "not good enough" belief comes up again.

Not sure what core limiting beliefs you have? Here's a great exercise to help you get familiar with them. Things is, once you can name them, how they show up in your life, and the subsequent impact, you can start to shift them.

So, get out your journal and do this exercise on core limiting beliefs.

IDENTIFYING CORE LIMITING BELIEFS

First write out your core limiting belief. You might have to really think about it. They are the thoughts and beliefs that keep you from asking for that promotion, or going after that relationship, or anything that keeps you "small" in some area of your life.

Here are some examples:

I am not good enough.
I am not smart enough.
I am a bad person.
I always have bad luck. It must be karma from a past life.
I always screw things up, so why even try.
I'm too lazy to succeed.
No one could ever love me, I'm just not lovable.

Now choose a core limiting belief that you want to release.
I'll use this one;
I do not have enough education (or the "right" education) to be a leader.

Next, write out the thoughts that play on repeat in your self-talk about this belief?
Eg. I don't have the "right" education, so no one will take me seriously.
Next, what feelings are associated with these negative thoughts?
I feel like an imposter in front of my team since many of them are more "educated" than me.

Now, what actions do you take (or not take) because of these feelings?
I go into people pleaser mode hoping that my team won't notice the lack of education.

Finally, what are the results of having these feelings.
I struggle to set solid boundaries with my team.

$\mathcal{S}$elf-Reflection & Awareness:
Core Limiting Beliefs

Core Limiting Belief?

What thoughts play on repeat in your self-talk about this belief?

What feelings are associated with these negative thoughts?

What actions do you take (or not take) because of these feelings?

What are the results of having these feelings.

3 Major Beliefs

First lesson

Over the years, there have been three core limiting beliefs that I had to uncover and walk through to see how they impacted my business. Then I had to learn how to heal and/or release them to step fully into the leader that I am today.

For me, I was in my first year as a CEO of a consulting firm in the gas, oil, chemical and petrochemical world when I realized that I was struggling with core limiting beliefs. I don't know if I would have called them that at the time. I just knew that I simply didn't believe that I was experienced or smart enough to run my business. On the surface, it didn't make sense because I have several degrees, including a master's in international business, and I speak multiple languages, so I knew that I was smart. However, I still didn't feel like I had the right to tell my employee, someone more experienced than me, how to do his job.

Have you ever been in this position? Do you question your right to tell someone what to do, even though you are the boss, or have knowledge that they don't have?

Thing is, if you don't feel like you are good enough, it won't matter how many degrees you have, or how much experience, you will still feel like it isn't your place to tell someone else what to do…you may find yourself feeling like an imposter.

This became my reality shortly after hiring an employee. It didn't take me long to realize that he and I were not in alignment with how I wanted to run my business. I struggled with telling him what to do and couldn't figure out why that was so difficult for me. After all, it is my business, I should be able to run it the way I see fit.

And then, when I did give him instructions on how I wanted to do things, he would agree, then he would do things the way he wanted anyway, saying, "that's how I've always done it."

When things came to a head and I made the decision to let him go, I allowed myself to be talked into giving him another chance. I say "allowed myself" because I was afraid of the conflict that was forthcoming, literally sick to my stomach. So, when he made all kinds of promises, complained that it wasn't fair, etc., I gave in with the caveat that he met all of my expectations without fail or it would be an immediate dismissal.

He agreed.

It didn't take long before it was clear that he wasn't going to change. If anything, he started to sabotage business relationships. I had to deal with my aversion to conflict and my fear of making a mistake and letting him go or risk my business.

I cried when I fired him; big ugly tears, even though I believed it was best for my business, and for me. But why did I struggle so much? This began the search for answers and the first step to dealing with core limiting beliefs.

I learned that there are subconscious beliefs that we develop early on and can be brought on by any number of things. In this case, the obvious one for me was from some sexual abuse that I had suffered as a child. It is logical that that period of my life would have a negative impact on me and still have subconscious murmurings of unworthiness.

What childhood events still impact you? Do you ever stop to consider what events, people, or even places still color your view of the world today, whether overtly or subliminally?

Perhaps you have worked with a therapist or done some work with a coach. What did you find? If not, what would you find? Are you afraid to look? I was. What makes you afraid?

These and other questions are the ones that started to circulate around my head.

I started to pay attention to my thoughts. To do so, I started journaling; sporadically at first, and then more consistently.

By the way, if you aren't journaling, it is a fabulous way to pay attention to the thoughts in your head that keep you feeling unworthy.

Journaling exercise – leadership fears

A good place to start is to simply write out your story. It doesn't have to be complicated. Write out your thoughts about what a good leader is and why you think you would be a good leader.

Next, write out all the fears that pop up when you think about stepping into a leadership role or a higher leadership role.

Read through those fears then put your journal down.

Put some music on and dance, shake, jump up and down, whatever feels good right now.

Now, pick up your journal and write out why those fears are silly, exaggerated, or unwarranted today.

For example, I had a belief that leadership was for men and my fear was that I simply could not lead because I wasn't wired that way.

After my dance session, I realized that the fear stemmed

from some childhood conditioning and that I knew of several women that were amazing leaders; Madeleine Albright, Bonnie Blair, Oprah Winfrey, Katie Couric, Angela Merkel, and Ruth Bader Ginsburg to name a few. On a personal level, the head of my university math department was also a woman. So, clearly this belief that women can't lead was a fallacy.

That led to the next fear, that I, personally, couldn't lead.

Another dance session later, I was able to recall, and document, several times that I successfully stepped into a leadership role; youth leader at church, bakery manager, and volunteer event coordinator for a couple of weddings.

This practice of 1. Write out the fear, 2. dance it out, then 3. write out why the fear is a story that I tell myself vs truth is one that I continue to practice today.

Second lesson

The second BIG lesson came when I had a client fire me for reasons that were outside of my control.

I had been working as a consultant with an international oil company for several years when a new corporate person joined their team. The first time I met this man, he walked into the room in which I was leading a team, sat down without saying a word, opened his computer and started typing.

My entire team stopped functioning and sat watching this man, incredulous at both his arrogance and his rudeness. We all assumed that it was the new corporate director of the process (we had been told he was coming), but none of us was sure.

I cleared my throat and introduced myself, then asked him who he was. He gave his name then told us to "carry on as though he wasn't there." So, I started back up with my team.

Occasionally he would ask a question. Then he would fall silent again, continuing to type on his computer, seemingly ignoring what we were doing.

Then he abruptly asked me, "can you please explain to me what it is you're doing?" I did. He then proceeded to tell me that I was doing my job incorrectly. It wasn't my fault, he said, just that I had been taught incorrectly. I stopped the team meeting.

To say I was upset would be an understatement.

Can you even imagine? I was so upset my hands were shaking. Have you ever had that happen? It sucks! Especially when you are standing in front of a room of people (and they were all men).

Over the next couple of years, we worked together quite closely and formed a professional alliance of sorts. When the CEO of that organization retired, the new leadership came in and let go of everyone from the old guard that was not in agreement with the new leadership.

The man I had been working with was one of those let go. Unfortunately, the alliance he and I had formed reflected on me, even though I was a paid consultant doing as I was told, and the new guard fired me as well.

This episode hit me hard. The man with whom I had had an alliance was difficult to work with. However, I had managed to form an uneasy truce with him. I didn't always agree with him but knew that I had to get along with him to continue supporting this client.

When he was fired, I was actually relieved…until they decided that I had to go as well.

I spent many sleepless nights going through everything in my head, replaying what I could have said to change the minds of the new leadership. Feeling like I had been targeted simply because of who I knew. Feeling like I was not given an opportunity to defend myself.

Have you ever had moments like this where you questioned what happened? It's easy to blame someone else, isn't it?

I started down the "blaming someone else" track until I realized that the feelings that I was feeling were reminiscent of events in my youth.

Thinking about those childhood events, it didn't seem logical that I felt the same way…at least, not at first. When I was a teen, I was bullied. I was bullied from 10 years old until I was out of high school by a group of girls. Whereas in my more recent situation, it was a group of men.

However, the feeling of not having a voice, not being able to defend myself, finding myself allied with someone that I thought could/would protect me but couldn't or didn't…all of that was the same. It didn't matter what I said, what I did, who stood up for me, or that my work was solid. I was fired. Just like in high school, it didn't matter what I said, what I did, who stood up for me or that I played by their rules, they bullied me…sometimes quite brutally.

After all was said and done, I was angry and scared. I couldn't believe that this client let me go. I had done so much work with and for them over the years.

I felt betrayed. But mostly, I felt like I had betrayed myself because I had become complacent in thinking that I wouldn't be fired because of the longevity of the relationship. In that complacency, I had gotten lazy, and I didn't have a great back-up.

This whole thing was like a punch in the gut.

I had to find a way to work through my feelings because they were all consuming and the meditation, dancing and journaling weren't working; at least not fast enough.

I went through my toolkit to find something that would help me.

What would you do?

You have an established way of dealing with stuff but then a bombshell gets dropped on you and somehow the old way of doing things doesn't seem adequate. You know?

I decided that I needed to do some inner child journeying. I had been reluctant to do this, but now it felt necessary.

Before I share this technique, I feel it necessary to let you know both what inner child journeying is, and why I was reluctant to do one.

An inner child journey is a healing modality, often done as a meditation, that takes you back to some event in your past in which a piece of your psyche was hurt, damaged, angered, or impacted in some negative manner. The goal is to reconnect with that part of yourself that might not have received the love and affection that was needed when you were younger.

So, going back to that point and "talking" to your younger version of you can be difficult at times. First, we don't always know what we will see or hear and so we can sometimes be surprised by what pops up. And second, if there was a lot of trauma in our lives, we can be afraid of remembering and therefore reliving the trauma. Not a fun idea and the impetus behind my reluctance to do an inner child journey.

However, the reason I opted to go ahead with one is that I had heard how healing it was. I had also been told that the point of completing a journey isn't to relive the trauma, it is to talk to that younger version of us that was hurt and help them heal.

Often just being 'seen and heard' is sufficient to release the energy, and therefore the trauma, of the event.

The journey itself only lasts 15-20 minutes, but the aftereffects, well, let's just say they can be life changing.

So, with that, I decided to do some journeying.

Inner Child Journey

Here is the meditation that I currently use; it is a variation of that first one. My suggestion is to read through it, record it on your phone, then sit back and listen. Do this meditation as often as feels right.

How do you feel?

Use the journal page provided to explore your experience with this meditation.

Inner Child Journey

Find a comfortable position, sitting or lying down.

Close your eyes.

Take three deep breaths; breathe in, breathe out.

Imagine that you step into an elevator, on the 10th floor.

Watch your finger push the button for the ground floor. Watch the numbers on the screen as they go down. As the elevator goes down, you feel your body relax.

9 - your breathing is getting deeper.

8 - your shoulders and neck are relaxing.

7 - your chest and arms are feeling relaxed

6 - your stomach and pelvis area are relaxing

5 - your legs are feeling heavy

4 - you relax even deeper

3 - the sound of my voice takes you even deeper

2 - the sounds around you take you even deeper and you are very relaxed

1 - your body is deeply relaxed.

The doors open to a beautiful garden and you step out. You notice a path leading through a dense forest.

You start down the path and look around.

You notice the swaying of some branches and feel a slight breeze on your face, the temperature of the air a slightly cool, comfortable temperature. You can hear birds singing and flitting through the trees and you notice butterflies flying around.

As you are walking, you notice that the ground is soft, your footsteps silent.

As you enter the woods, the temperature cools, the sounds of the birds change slightly, as if calling you.

You continue walking, noticing your surroundings; the sway of the tree branches, the silence broken only by the sound of the rustling of leaves and singing of birds.

As you are walking you come into an open meadow filled with bright,

fragrant flowers. In the center you see a group of people.

You feel like you know them, but they are too far away.

As you draw closer, you realize they are all you, different versions of you.

You sit and look around, recognizing yourself in the

faces of each being looking back at you.

You ask, "who is responsible for this situation?" (Name the specific situation).

Someone steps forward. Just notice them. Smile.

They may be hurt, angry, or afraid, so, look at them

tenderly, lovingly and gently ask,

'Who are you?'

Listen as they tell you their name. Perhaps it is a younger version of you.

Perhaps an emotion that you have buried. Either is ok.

Ask them, 'Tell me how you are involved, and what you are trying to accomplish.'

Are they trying to protect you in some way?

Chances are they are trying to keep you safe in some way. So, take a

few minutes to listen to what they are saying.

Now, invite them to go with you to the top of a nearby mountain. You can walk, skip,

hop, ride a magic carpet or whatever feels right at this moment.

At the top, show them what you have already created and

the vision that you have for your life.

Thank them for what they've done for you thus far and invite them to a new role. How

could they shift their focus to assist you in achieving your vision?

For example, if they were more critical of things in your life, maybe they could

become more discerning and help you set better boundaries.

Once it is clear what their new role will be in your life, tell them thank you and how

much you love them. Then hug them and allow them to become a part of you again.

Place your hands on your heart and just feel the love for a minute.

Now, slowly wiggle your toes, stretch, and gently open your eyes.

Self-Reflection & Awareness:

Inner Child Journey

Who did I meet today? What was their name? What did they look like?

_____

_____

_____

What is my inner child trying to help me with? What message did they have for me?

_____

_____

_____

_____

What is the new role that they are taking in my life?

_____

_____

_____

_____

How will this change or improve in my life?

_____

_____

_____

_____

_____

_____

When you've gone through an inner child journey, it is common to feel some elation, after all, you've just healed a part of yourself that has been hurting for how many years?

For me, that first time was pretty amazing.

I cried throughout my first inner child journey. Let's just say, I'm not a crier. However, they were tears that had waited a long time to be released.

A small, docile, mousy version of me stepped forward, afraid to show herself. Her whole goal to "help me" was to keep me from being a target. She had been trying to keep me 'small' to keep me safe from cruel words, being laughed at, and overall hateful criticism.

At the end, when I asked her what role she would like to play in the greater vision of my life, she opted to remain discerning of people and situations that came into my life.

After my inner child journey, I was able to look at the situation that brought me here and see where, in aligning myself to this person, I had been trying to use my colleague as a shield. Unfortunately, it backfired when he was let go.

However, I took the lesson I learned from it and moved forward creating stronger alliances and healthier relationships with clients. My younger self has held up her end and I have more discernment than before.

Third Lesson

The largest piece of the "enoughness" puzzle came later. It was a doozy. I had to go through layers of emotion to unbury this very core limiting belief. It happened when a 28 year friendship exploded. I had called this woman my best friend for 28 years, and then one day, I realized that I was her friend; she wasn't mine. A mutual friend said, "You can't really be friends with a narcissist, and she's a narcissist. You can only learn how to handle them in a way that is not damaging to your soul."

She was right. For years I had known that the relationship was very one-sided, and yet, I continued to allow it. I had simply limited the amount of time I spent with her at any given time. When the relationship blew up, I started to look at why and how I had ended up in a relationship like this, especially since I was coaching other women on how to set boundaries.

I breathed. It was during a breathwork session that I remembered abuse from my childhood that involved my sister. She was verbally, emotionally, and sometimes physically abusive. Talking to an adult did not stop the abuse. I was told "it takes two to fight." When you are told that you are part of the problem, even when you are simply sitting and reading a book, you start to believe that you are part of the problem.

I dissociated from the abuse which led to a core belief that something was "wrong with me", later allowing me to be in this narcissistic friendship. After all, if someone was willing to befriend me when clearly there was "something wrong with me" then I should be thankful. Right?

Are you following me? Complicated, I know.

It took me several months to unravel the emotions of both my childhood abuse and the correlation between that and allowing myself to be caught up in the web of a narcissist.

I decided to do some forgiveness work; specifically, forgiveness letters.

I wrote several forgiveness letters.

I wrote one to my sister and my friend.

I wrote them to my parents.

I wrote them to the bullies from high school.

And I wrote them to myself for allowing myself to be in this position again.

I know the last one might sound weird. However, I felt that I had let myself down. So, I wrote myself a forgiveness letter.

The letters had a rhythm.

Forgiveness letters

As you are going through this, really allow your feelings to surface. Go into as much detail as you need to be able to release the energy, the thoughts, emotions and beliefs that you've held onto for so long.

At first, you might find yourself holding back. That's ok. In the second of third iteration of the letter, you will find yourself truly opening up and expressing your feelings. That's why I would encourage you to do this 2-3 times.

Start with:

I'm writing this letter with the intention of….

(telling you how I feel, releasing all of this toxicity, healing myself…etc.)

I sometimes feel angry about…

(your being an ass, how you abused me, how you withhold your love from me…etc.)

I sometimes feel hurt about…

(how you speak to me, how rejected I feel, how you cheated on me…etc.)

Something I feel sad about is…

(how good it could have been if…, how you didn't value me, that our kids saw your sh*tty behavior…)

I regret…

(not leaving you sooner, not telling my family about the abuse sooner, that I gave you so much of my time…)

3 things I would like from you now are…

(space, for me to be able to release the chord between us, an apology…etc.).

You can do this several times, writing several drafts to the same person if need be. I have used this, throughout the years, to work through forgiveness on a variety of topics.

It is amazing the power of forgiveness. I had been told forgiveness is not about the other person. I had even repeated that phrase a hundred times to my kids. Still, until I did this work, I didn't truly understand how much it really is about releasing the energy of the other person from your system. In forgiving both this "friend" and my sister, I was actually letting go of the story that had kept me in the emotional web for so long.

What story are you repeating over and over that keeps you locked in a cycle? Are you ready to let it go? What story do you have to let go of to fully embrace your life? I'm telling you; forgiveness is a powerful way to do that. Give it a try!

Self-Reflection & Awareness:

Forgiveness Letters

I'm writing this letter with the intention of....

_____

_____

_____

I sometimes feel angry about...

_____

_____

_____

_____

I sometimes feel hurt about...

_____

_____

_____

_____

Something I feel sad about is...

_____

_____

_____

_____

_____

_____

Self-Reflection & Awareness:

Forgiveness Letter cont.

I regret...

_____

_____

_____

_____

3 things I need from you now are...

_____

_____

_____

_____

_____

_____

_____

_____

_____

_____

_____

_____

_____

_____

_____

_____

_____

2

EMBODYING MASCULINE AND FEMININE ENERGIES AS A CEO

B ecoming a CEO requires a dynamic blend of both masculine and feminine energies—a balance of assertiveness and intuition, structure and creativity, decisiveness and collaboration. The most effective leaders integrate both of these energies rather than favoring one over the other.

Masculine energy, which is most often associated with drive, logic, and strategic execution, is crucial for leadership. It manifests in a CEO's ability to make bold decisions, take calculated risks, and establish clear direction. A CEO must exude confidence, set ambitious goals, and execute plans with precision. This energy fuels discipline, resilience, and focus, which are essential in a competitive business landscape.

However, solely operating from masculine energy can lead to burnout, rigidity, and disconnection from employees and customers. This is where feminine energy becomes vital. Feminine energy embodies empathy, intuition, adaptability, and collaboration—qualities that help CEOs build strong company cultures, nurture relationships, and lead with emotional intelligence. In an era where employee engagement and brand authenticity are crucial, tapping into deep listening, flexibility, and inclusivity fosters loyalty and innovation.

Bringing Balance

A truly successful CEO integrates both energies seamlessly. They trust their instincts while making data-driven decisions, maintain confidence without arrogance, and create a vision that is both ambitious and sustainable. This balance enables them to command respect while inspiring trust, driving both performance and well-being within the organization.

Ultimately, embracing both masculine and feminine energies isn't about gender, it's about wholeness. The most influential CEOs cultivate a leadership style that is both powerful and compassionate, ensuring long-term success in business and personal fulfillment.

They also embody leadership. In other words, leadership is at the core of their being. They ARE a leader; they don't just wear the hat of a leader.

Do you know what I mean? Do you "put on your leadership hat"? How does that make you feel? Like an imposter? If you embrace leadership as *who you are*, then leadership becomes your mindset; and that's embodiment.

Learning to lean into the feminine

Here's my experience with this…

When I first started my consulting business, RISK, I was quite comfortable working in a masculine environment. I had always had a propensity for math and science which are fields dominated by men.

I remember it clearly; it was our first Christmas party. My husband and I were on our way when my son called and started in on me about his sister. He felt that I was not being very nice, in fact, he straight up felt that I was being a b*tch. He believed that I should be helping her more and that my recent decision not to allow her in the house was too much.

He had no idea what we had done for her and I told him so.

At that point, he started yelling at me.

I hung up the phone.

Back story is that our daughter was a drug addict. At the point at which this conversation happened, she had two children of which my husband and I had custody. In addition to raising her children, we had paid for apartments, hotels, and cars over the years. We had even put her through rehab, to no avail.

The conversation with our son was because she had asked for some help because she was about to get evicted. This time, we refused. Too many lies had been told.

That evening, as we sat and had dinner at an amazing restaurant with our team I thought about the conversation. One of the men on the team was a heavy drinker. As the evening progressed, I watched him drink and thought about the amount of patience and compassion that I had for him versus our daughter. I realized that while I had had a large amount of patience with her, there was also sadness, anger, judgement, shame, and blame, and very little compassion.

Where had I lost the compassion for her?

I knew that I had to work through my feelings. I also knew that doing so meant that I had to get better in touch with my feminine energy, or the nurturing, compassionate side of my being. I just didn't know how, AND I was scared. I was afraid that getting in touch with my feelings would open a floodgate that I couldn't control.

Have you felt this fear? It is paralyzing, isn't it? The paralysis can be especially bad because society says that we, as women, are already too emotional, and that's when we are closed off, numb and shut down!! I could only imagine what was about to unfold.

I started exploring my emotions.

I quickly discovered that it was difficult for me to do. I had locked away so many feelings, replacing them with someone else's stories about what was acceptable for me to feel, or be. I had heard, "Rene' you should…" so many times in my life…that I did.

However, unlocking the door to my emotions was more challenging than I anticipated. I didn't know how.

Have you had that happen where you make up your mind that you are going to do something, but you don't have a clue how to go about doing it?

Well, I am first and foremost a lover of learning, so I started to research compassion, and emotional aware-ness, and why women feel emotionally stuck. What I found is what I already knew. My childhood trauma and the ensuing years of "we don't talk about stuff like that" had left me bereft of feeling any connection with my daughter now that she was using. There was too much judgment.

I had to forgive her, and me. I also had to learn how to feel; feel compassion, connection, and emotions, all emotions, not just those I am supposed to feel.

I used the forgiveness letters from above, which helped, but they were not enough. At first, I struggled to understand what was happening. The forgiveness letters had done so much for me in other areas, why not here?

After doing more research and going deeper into everything, I realized how "out of my body I was". The inability to feel, the numbness and surface level calmness were strong indicators of what is called dissociation. Basically, we "check out" of our bodies and put a smile on our face.

Women are particularly good at this. How many times were you told, "be a good girl", or "good girls don't behave that way", or "you're so emotional, calm down"?

That familial and societal conditioning has affected many of us. Well, for me, it had to change. I wanted to *feel*! Something! Anything!

I started exploring different ways to "get back in my body".

I found a couple of variations of a 5 senses process to help me awaken my senses. I took those and combined them to help me to get back in my body and feel my emotions, thus beginning the awakening and embodiment of the feminine.

5 senses journey

Here's my variation for those of you who are struggling with feeling in touch with your emotions. You might choose to write in your journal with different color pens.

See - notice 5 things in your immediate area. Take note of the color, shape, texture(s) and how they make you feel. Where is the feeling in your body? Just observe. Release any judgement that might come up.

For example, I am looking at a photo of my mother and stepfather, they are both smiling. The picture has a matte gold frame and there's a bit of a glare on the glass on the left side. I feel a tightness and a warmth in my chest. My inclination is to question or judge the tightness and want to know why it's there. However, by simply observing, allowing, and feeling, the tightness releases.

Make observations for four more things that you see.

Hear - notice 4 things that you hear. Are the sounds soft and subtle, or harsh and blatant, or somewhere in between? Are the sounds outside or inside? How do the sounds make you feel?

For example, I hear a dishwasher running in the other room. The sound is muted and rhythmic. When I listen to it, I feel a softness in my belly.

Now observe 3 more sounds.

Touch/Feel - notice 3 things that you feel. These would be sensory things as opposed to emotional things.

For example, I feel my sweater against my arms. The texture is slightly coarse and soft. It makes me warm, leaving me feeling a lightness in my heart and solar plexus area.

Make another two observations.

Smell - notice 2 things you smell.

For example, I smell the laundry soap on my shirt. The smell is a strong, fresh smell. It makes me feel clean, and happy, like sunshine.

Now see if you smell one more thing.

Finally taste - notice one thing.

For example, I taste the sweetness of the Trader Joe's dark chocolate peanut butter cup that I ate 10-15 minutes ago. It tastes sweet and salty at the same time. It makes my heart sing.

Do this exercise a couple of times a week. Change it up! Feel 5 things, smell 4, see 3, hear 2 and taste 1. If you have limited time, go through each of the senses once.

This exercise will help you get into and stay in your body. It's fantastic!

Self-Reflection & Awareness:
5 Senses

5 things I see and how they make me feel is...

_____

_____

_____

_____

_____

4 things I hear are...

_____

_____

_____

3 things I feel are...

_____

_____

_____

2 things I smell are...

_____

_____

_____

1 thing I taste is...

_____

_____

Learning to lean into the masculine

It was after I started to lean into my intuition more and "listening" to my body that I began to embrace feminine energy.

And with that, I rejected the "get it done" mantra of the masculine energy. This idea of leading from the feminine led to me choosing to make decisions from a state of 'what feels good', or "leading from the heart".

This went well at first. Unfortunately, it didn't take long before things in my business started to fall apart. It didn't make sense! I was listening to my intuition, making decisions about what felt right and leading from a place of compassion. Why, then, was business going down?

Maybe you've been there, where things don't make sense? You are making decisions based on your "gut", treating your employees and clients with compassion and caring, careful of the words that you use lest you be seen as aggressive, insensitive, or mean, and yet, things aren't going well?

So, again, I started looking for answers, going deeper in my research looking into leadership, compassionate leadership, and the impacts of both masculine and feminine energies on leadership.

What I found is that by embracing only my feminine energies, my leadership was back out of balance. By first allowing feminine energy into my life, then repudiating the masculine, my business was impacted because of the imbalance of my leadership. It was failing due to the lack of discipline, and goal oriented direction; more "masculine" traits.

One of the ways that this imbalance reared its ugly head is the following.

I had given employees guidelines, but not hard lines. With a small team of 17 people, mostly engineers, I expected them to be the intelligent adults that I knew them to be and follow my guidelines.

They didn't.

Timesheets weren't getting put in on time making it a challenge to bill appropriately, files weren't posted for internal review in a timely manner, communication with clients was often delayed, and report deadlines were missed.

Another thing that happened is that my people-pleasing tendencies from my childhood showed up with a vengeance! I believed that "leading from the heart" or embracing my feminine energy meant that I couldn't set good boundaries, so, rather than tell them "Thou shalt get this done" my attitude was "could you pretty please?"

This exacerbated the lack of structure that my team had.

Can you just feel the frustration and resentment that was being generated in both directions?

As I studied more about masculine and feminine energies, it led to an understanding that I was now leaning too heavily into my feminine energy.

To offset this, I stepped back into my masculine energy somewhat, creating a more balanced energy within. This led to me setting goals with actionable steps for me and my team. It also meant getting *really* clear about why this goal was important to me.

By creating processes for my business to help keep things on track, and still allowing for compassion and intuition, I found that the symbiotic relationships of the two were a powerful way to lead.

Goal setting

A powerful way to set actionable goals is to start with your top goal.

Break it down into monthly goals.

Then weekly,

And finally daily.

Then add how you will celebrate achieving this goal.

For example;

I wanted to create a book that would help and inspire other women in their leadership journey so that they could become the CEO of *their* lives.

I wanted to write a book and publish it in 2025.

Monthly would be to complete 100-150 pages a month.

That would be between 25,000 and 37,500 words.

Weekly would be 37.5 pages or 6,250 - 9,375 words.

Daily would be just over 5 pages or between 892 and 1339 pages.

I intend to celebrate the publishing of this book with a big online party with all of my FB friends and also to go to dinner with my husband at my favorite restaurant.

Learning to balance masculine and feminine

The last piece of embodying masculine and feminine energies came in understanding the difference between wounded and healed energies, or what I like to call distorted and divine energies, what they look like and how they manifest themselves in our leadership.

After shifting into a more balanced state, I thought I had it all figured out.

You know how it is. You learn something, then you think, "Ah, yes, that is the answer."

Well, it wasn't "all figured out."

Things smoothed back out once I got clear with my goals, yes, but…not for long.

It was right about this point in my life that I started a second business.

I had several women that I had met in various arenas that were asking for mentorship, coaching, and support. So, it seemed like a good idea to start an actual business for coaching on the side.

I got myself a coach to help me get things set up.

During that time, I learned that I look at things differently than a lot of people. My coach was constantly telling me, "Rene', I never thought of it like that." We became friends and looked at going into business together. The business idea was hers, and the people on the project were her choice. All good.

However, when one of the women questioned her place on the team and I volunteered to help her step into her power, the woman on lead immediately took exception to my offer. It wasn't a week before she cancelled the project and after that, we spoke only one more time.

How many times have you had something like this occur, where you offer to help but someone else's "smallness" got projected onto you and you were accused of "trying to take over", or being a "know it all", or better yet, being arrogant?

This experience would repeat itself several more times over a 5 or 6 year period. Another person would want to collaborate on something, but they would end up pulling out for one reason or another, or I would.

I began to doubt myself again. Wouldn't you?

I believed myself to be a reasonable person, agreeable about most things, willing to compromise on almost everything, but still the collaborative projects that I pursued continued to fall through.

Then, when the unthinkable happened, unthinkable to me, anyway, and my friendship of 28 years came to a very abrupt ending, I went into a deep depression. For 28 years I had nurtured this friendship, taking care to always be there for my friend and her family, often flying a lot of miles for 2 or 3 days for events that were important to my friend, baby showers, birthdays, studio openings, moving parties, etc.

I mentioned this breakup in the last section. Well, during this period of exploration, the question about these collaborations also came up.

And after I had done forgiveness work around my friendship, I found there was another layer that had to be addressed, another layer that I uncovered.

I was in my masculine and feminine energies, yes, but they were my wounded masculine and feminine energies. My woundedness didn't allow me to fully embrace the positive aspects of the masculine and feminine energies.

So, here I want to give you a little more information about what I mean. Both masculine and feminine energies have a "positive" and a "negative" component to them. Think about it. There are men and women that are admirable, honest, caring, etc., and there are some that are mean-spirited, aggressive, and manipulative.

So, a woman who is in her wounded feminine energy may attract narcissistic people, people who are emotionally unavailable because they believe they are unlovable. They may also be overly critical of themselves and others, thus coming across as manipulative or judgmental. This is often a defense mechanism to hide their insecurities.

Then, a woman in her wounded masculine energy may have trust issues, be passive aggressive, and constantly seek external validation. They may also believe that feminine behavior is supposed to be passive, and therefore either become people pleasers or go the opposite directions becoming pit bulls.

Do any of these hit home? I'm betting at least one or two of them do.

During my months of depression, I really looked at myself and *all* of my relationships.

My 28 year "friendship" had been very one-sided. I was her friend, she wasn't mine. She was/is a narcissist. I was people pleasing, allowing her to dictate the rules of our relationship. Because she had to feed her narcissism, I was needed, feeding my desire or need to feel lovable.

This led to resentment on my part, passive aggressive behavior on both parts, and lots of self-judgment.

How many relationships have you had, or do you have in which you feel you are not valued? Listen to your body.

Upon further reflection, I began to grasp that in several of my other relationships over the years, I was very much a people pleaser, or I was critical, (more of myself than the other person…still…), or I believed I wasn't good enough for the relationship. There was also some "judginess" on my part and I'm sure some projection.

These honest reflections sucked! Not going to lie to you. When you look in a mirror and realize that you might have been part of the problem…well, let's just say it might not be fun.

Obviously, this had to change. It was not what I wanted; not who I wanted to be.

Rescript and pivoting

I went back to my tool chest of modalities and found two that I felt would be most helpful, rescripting and pivoting.

Here's how they work in my world. (Remember, I modify things to fit me and my personality, making sure to retain the critical elements.)

First, write out your story about what it is you want to change. It can be about friendships, leadership, finances, etc.

Take some time to really get into details of who, what, when, why, where, and how.

Put the story down for a couple of days.

Now go back and read what you have written.

After you've read it. Reread it with a colored pen in your hand.

Circle every negative sounding word you come across.

For example, if you are writing about finances and you are recalling how things were while growing up, you may have written something like this:

Growing up, we never had money. We were always struggling to make ends meet. My parents never took me to the movies or let me have a bike or anything normal kids did. etc.

So, in reading this, you might say to me, "Rene', this was my reality, I'm not saying anything negative." To which I'd reply. I understand.

Still, there are words in this story that you keep telling yourself, which are negative, or have a negative connotation.

Never.

Always struggling.

Normal. (Implying *you* weren't normal).

Circle these words or phrases. Do it throughout your story.

Next, rewrite your story using neutral or positive words. So, it might look something like this:

Growing up, we had *little* money. We had to get creative to make ends meet. My parents didn't take me to the movies or buy me a bike like other kids. My parents did this so that they could be assured that we would have enough money for necessities. etc.

Do you see how different that feels? You can do this about virtually any subject matter you want. Needless to say, I did quite a bit of 'rescripting'.

Rewriting your story creates new beliefs. Creating new beliefs creates new realities. With new realities comes new ways of behaving, speaking, leading, and loving.

The beautiful thing about rescripting is that you are not lying about your story. You are simply looking at it through a different lens. Often, looking through a different lens you learn things about yourself and your family that you may not have realized before, and light-bulbs start going off about where some of your core limiting beliefs came from.

(Are you seeing the circle?)

The other part of what I did to address this is pivoting. Full confession, I do this slightly differently than I was taught. I was taught to pivot mentally. For example, when you catch yourself telling your old version of your story, *mentally* pivot yourself to your newer version.

Me? I physically pivot myself. If I am sitting in my chair, I will turn it so that I am looking at something different, literally giving me a different perspective.

This is both a physical and mental check for me. I have found it to be far more effective for me than doing just a mental pivot.

Try it! Then let me know what you think!

Self-Reflection & Awareness:

Rescripting

Your story

_____

_____

_____

_____

_____

_____

_____

_____

_____

_____

_____

_____

_____

_____

_____

_____

_____

_____

_____

_____

_____

_____

_____

_____

Self-Reflection & Awareness:

Rescripting

Your new story

_____

_____

_____

_____

_____

_____

_____

_____

_____

_____

_____

_____

_____

_____

_____

_____

_____

_____

_____

_____

_____

_____

_____

3

TEAM DYNAMICS

THE IMPORTANCE OF TEAM DYNAMICS IN BECOMING A CEO

S trong team dynamics are essential for any CEO looking to build a high-performing organization. A CEO's success is not just about individual leadership but also about how well they facilitate connection, collaboration, communication, and trust within their team. Understanding and managing team dynamics can be the difference between a thriving company and one plagued by inefficiency and disengagement.

One of the key roles of a CEO is to cultivate a culture of trust and accountability. When employees feel valued, heard, and empowered, they are more likely to contribute innovative ideas and take ownership of their work. A CEO must, therefore, foster an environment where team members can collaborate effectively, resolve conflicts constructively, and work towards shared goals.

Additionally, strong team dynamics boost productivity and morale. When employees trust their leaders and colleagues, they are more engaged and motivated. A CEO who recognizes the strengths of each team member and leverages those strengths effectively can drive performance while maintaining a positive workplace culture. They see diverse perspectives as a positive and leverage them to create more well-rounded strategies and solutions.

Poor team dynamics, on the other hand, can lead to miscommunication, inefficiency, a toxic environment, and high turnover. Therefore, a CEO must actively address conflicts, encourage collaboration, and lead by example in fostering a respectful and inclusive environment.

Ultimately, the ability to build and sustain strong team dynamics is a defining trait of a great CEO. Leadership is not about doing everything alone, it's about empowering others, aligning efforts, and creating a vision that unites the team toward success.

Would you agree with the importance of the CEO's role in defining the team dynamics within an organization? And can you see why all of the inner work that you focused on in the first two sections of this book matters so much in how you lead?

It matters in many ways, not the least of which is how you respond to versus interact with your team. It also helps you recognize some of these same core limiting beliefs that you may have within other people so that you can more effectively manage your team.

I would define team dynamics as the interaction between you and your team members, including how they respond (or react to) clients, each other and the impact thereon.

Toxic employees

Let me give an example.

I had an employee that was extremely knowledgeable in a particular area within our business. Clients sought him out.

Problem was, he was also extremely negative, in-house. We would have a meeting and all he would do is complain about the client du jour. It was so toxic that other employees took on the same belief system about the client before they even worked with them. They'd go into a project with the *expectation* of all the negative things that they had heard and would therefore come back with similar stories.

I also did work with this client. A lot of it. I loved the client and would counteract the negativity with a different version. Problem was that this employee did a lot of the training of new employees. So, new folks heard more from him than me.

How this played out in the workplace is that the employees that bought into the negative story were less responsive to the client and had a more difficult time getting reports in on time. Whereas, with other clients, this issue did not exist.

I knew that I had to find a way to address this.

At first, I found myself willing to blame the employee for his bad behavior. However, my dad had a saying, "if you are pointing fingers at someone, look down, there are three pointing back at you."

In other words, I had to take responsibility for my role in allowing this sort of thing to continue.

I could, one, fire him. That didn't make sense. He was sought out by clients, even with his lackadaisical attitude in responding to them.

I could, two, remove him from the trainer role. That

also didn't make sense due to his knowledge and my availability to step into that role.

Or, three, I could figure out a way to shift the energy of our team meetings, and work with him to shift his energy during his training.

I started with the team meetings. First, I provided more structure for the meetings, setting up training sessions, and discussions on how to manage a team.

Next, I had some discussions around overall attitudes towards and about clients, encouraging everyone to remember that our clients are people trying to do their jobs the best they can within the constraints they were given.

And finally, I had some private conversations with my trainer about his attitude. I learned that he was dealing with a lot of stress at home, including recently meeting his biological family.

It explained a lot. He was dealing with the trauma of "not being wanted" and it was showing up in his work and home life creating a lot of stress.

The reality is, I could have gotten angry, I could have been accusatory, I could have pointed fingers about unhappy clients, late reports, etc. instead, I chose compassion.

I have learned to "read" people through how their energy shows up in my body. This, I have found, has proven to be the most effective tool when managing other people.

First, you have to understand where your emotions show up in your body.

Journaling exercise - feelings

Get out a pen and piece of paper. Then, think about some different emotions. If just thinking about an emotion is difficult, try thinking about something that makes you feel a certain way. Then notice where you feel sensations in your body.

For example, think, sad. If necessary, think about a sad situation. What do you feel? Where do you feel it? Maybe you feel a tightness in your chest. Perhaps, you feel it in your throat. Some people feel a warmth, or a coldness somewhere in their body. Whatever you feel, and wherever you feel it is uniquely yours. Write it down in your journal.

Now try anger

Joy

Fear

Pity

Judgement

Compassion

Pay attention to the subtle nuances you feel. For example, I feel sadness as a tightness across my chest. Pity, for me, is a knot in my stomach with the tightness in my chest, and compassion is both the tightness in my chest while also feeling open hearted. Weird, I know.

But this awareness is why I was able to have a very constructive conversation with my employee. I felt compassion. This told me that he needed someone to see and hear him without judgment.

I did that.

He opened up. The conversation that followed was a powerful reminder that we all have trauma. Some of us are starting to understand how much that impacts us and are taking appropriate actions. Others are *so* unaware. This reminder made me even more appreciative of the tools that I have learned.

When the conversation was over, he thanked me profusely for taking the time to allow him to just talk through everything and really listen to him without judgment. Once I understood what was going on, I was glad to have taken the time to do so.

We then talked a little about some of the challenges that

I was seeing at work and how I might best support him as he navigated this emotional minefield. When the call ended, he was recommitted to the company, which changed his energy during meetings, responses to clients, and his overall attitude.

Self-Reflection & Awareness:
Feeling Your Feelings

Choose your emotion. For example, sadness.

_____

Where do you feel this in your body, ie. throat, shoulders, solar plexus?

_____

_____

_____

What else do you feel, ie. warmth, coldness, hardness?

_____

_____

_____

Pay attention to subtleties, ie. tightness across your chest, a hole or knot in your stomach.

_____

_____

_____

Repeat with other emotions.

_____

_____

_____

_____

_____

_____

_____

Communication truths

This episode reminded me of an earlier event in my business, one in which I had had to navigate my own feelings around what an employee said to me.

She was a junior engineer, very young, and very eager to learn. She was also like a sponge, learning things very quickly, excited to be on our team, traveling, and dealing with clients from different companies and even different industries.

After about two years, we were traveling together on a project so that I could start training her on some higher level work. During our trip we had the opportunity to have a long conversation about how things were going, how she liked things, opportunities, etc.

During that conversation, I had the feeling that she was holding back. When I asked her what she was really feeling, she was hesitant to speak frankly.

And then, she did.

She told me about how she felt overwhelmed by some of the assignments that she had been given and that my communication with her about the assignments was lacking. I was surprised, to say the least. I had felt that she was getting great training from our trainer at the time. We had communicated some, but she was not a direct report to me. However, I had given her a special project to work on with an open ended approach. In other words, I let her know what outcome I was looking for, but did not dictate how she put it together. My thought was that she is intelligent and having the freedom to approach it as she desired would be appreciated.

I was wrong.

It left her feeling like she was "flapping in the wind".

We talked at length.

I discovered that she found me to be very intimidating and unapproachable.

I was shocked. I prided myself on being open and accessible to all of my employees. Hearing someone accuse me of being unapproachable…well…not only was I shocked, but I was also hurt, and confused.

How could I have gotten everything so wrong?

Have you ever looked in a mirror and seen one person only to discover that everyone else saw another?

It's unsettling, isn't it?

I started to question myself about everything. I even did this thing where I reached out to several people I knew and asked them how they saw me.

Like, really, it upset me a lot!

I found, in a book I was reading, a process that I really liked. I took and modified it (as always) to suit me, my learning style, and my end goals.

It helped me get clarity on how I presented myself, thus helping me to ensure that it matched how I saw myself.

It goes like this:

Divine/Distorted language

Take a piece of paper and lay it out in landscape mode.

Create 4 columns.

1. Write the Distorted (Negative) Masculine in the far-left hand column and Distorted Feminine in the far-right hand column.

2. Write Divine (Positive) Masculine in the center-left hand column and Divine (Positive) Feminine in the center-right hand column.

3. List as many qualities or behaviors as you can think of for both the Outer columns. These are the negative aspects and behaviors that leaders display.

4. Next list as many of the qualities or behaviors that you can think of for the Inner columns. These are the positive qualities a leader can have and display.

5. Circle the qualities that you employ and/or embody. Do they match the ones that you want to embody? If not, take a look and see, where are your triggers? What language are you using that keeps you in this behavior?

Journaling exercise – distorted energy

Journaling exercise: Where am I in my distorted energy? What triggers lead me to distortion? Am I willing to pivot?

$\mathcal{S}$elf-Reflection & Awareness:
Distorted vs Divine Energies

1. Write the Distorted (Negative) Masculine in the far-left hand column and Distorted Feminine in the far-right hand column.

2. Write Divine (Positive) Masculine in the center-left hand column and Divine (Positive) Feminine in the center-right hand column.

3. List as many qualities or behaviors as you can think of for both the Outer columns. These are the negative aspects and behaviors that leaders display.

4. Next list as many of the qualities or behaviors that you can think of for the Inner columns. These are the positive qualities a leader can have and display.

5. Circle the qualities that you employ and/or embody. Do they match the ones that you want to embody? If not, take a look and see, where are your triggers? What language are you using that keeps you in this behavior?

DISTORTED MASCULINE	DIVINE MASCULINE	DIVINE FEMININE	DISTORTED FEMININE
Aggressive Controlling	Assertive Does	Discerning Friendly	Manipulate Gossipy

So, what does all of this have to do with team dynamics? Well, if you see yourself in a certain way that is different from others, it creates discord.

And when you multiply that by however many people are on your team and you get, well…chaos.

Something had to be done. And as I've discovered, all real lasting change starts from within.

So, once you've completed the above exercise, you can start to pay attention to the energy of what you are saying, not only the words, but also the energy behind the words.

Then, if you are trying to get a point across, you may realize that instead of being assertive, you are, in fact, being aggressive because the energy behind your words is more aggressive. Why? If you feel you have to prove something to someone, there may be a bit of desperation, or frustration in your energy field. If that's the case, your energy may come across as aggressive.

Therefore, making sure that your energy field is clear is imperative. You can do this through dance or movement, or there are several breath techniques.

My favorite for this is boxed breathing. It calms your nervous system down so that you can deliver your words with the energy with which you wish to deliver them.

Box breathing

Box breathing is simple.

Breathe in for a count of 5.

Hold for a count of 5.

Breathe out for a count of 5.

Hold for 5.

Do this 4 or 5 times.

That's it.

This episode, coupled with the memory of the past event, reminded me of why I started my business. I had started my own company to lead in a different manner, with heart, integrity and compassion, as well as with strength. I wanted to empower my employees to be the best version of themselves while serving our clients with the highest quality and integrity.

Somewhere along the way, things had gotten sidetracked, I had gotten sidetracked.

Ever been sidetracked? It's easy to be distracted by everything that may be going on in your life. No need to beat yourself up over it, it happens. When it happens, acknowledge it and move forward.

Time to get back on track.

First, I had to be clear about my values. Were they even the same as when I started? I had changed so much over the years that I wasn't sure. What I was sure of is that I had to get clear in order to move forward in both businesses.

How many times have you had to reset, refocus and realign?

Core values

I sat down and started to write out everything that was important to me, in my personal and professional life. I read through it asking myself where I could be clearer. I continued to add details until it felt complete.

Next, I asked myself what values must I embody for this life to become a reality?

Then, I asked myself which ones were missing or needed augmenting, challenging myself to be really honest with myself.

Because, let's face it, if things were going to change, the only way it was going to happen is if I was honest about what had to change.

BTW (by the way), this little exercise took me almost a week to complete.

Regaining the clarity about both my values and goals provided me with a path forward for both businesses.

I highly recommend you do something along those lines for you.

But what does all of this inner work have to do with team dynamics, you ask?

Confidence.

If you have dealt with your trauma, healed core limiting beliefs and unresolved hurts, you have more confidence to deal with others.

You also have more compassion when addressing people, allowing them to feel seen, heard, and appreciated.

So, then, when you have to have the difficult conversations, you aren't avoiding them for fear of "hurting someone's feelings." You are having the conversations to resolve an issue so that everyone can show up more authentically.

Or, when you are in a meeting and have to "manage" a difficult person in the room, you don't take their verbal attack so personally because you understand that this person has some kind of trauma in their closet that they haven't dealt with yet.

So, now let's focus on the team, in team dynamics.

We all have this vision of only working with people we like, who think like us, or at least "get us". However, when we limit ourselves to that, we are limiting our growth. Working with people that we may not like a lot, or that think very differently than we do, or pushing us out of our comfort zone are people that push us to grow.

Think about it like this, if you have someone on your team that is "quirky" and with whom you really don't click, but they have a unique approach to doing things, they may come up with solutions that you and your "crew" wouldn't have thought of because of "groupthink".

Now, I'm not saying to work with difficult or toxic people, I'm saying find someone that is good at what they do, make sure they are aligned with your views, and then let them do their jobs. If you've done your inner work, you will have the confidence to be able to communicate effectively with this person.

Having your core values solidly in the forefront of everything you do makes it easier to hire someone in alignment with those values, thus helping you to build a team that has the same values, even if they don't agree with you, or communicate differently than you do.

It also makes it easier to delegate, train, mentor, and make decisions that may be unpopular within your team, all necessary components of team dynamics, just not the focus of this book.

Self-Reflection & Awareness:
Core Values

Personal life goals

What values must I embody to make this a reality?

What values must I develop to achieve this? (which am I lacking?)

Daily steps to achieve goal

How I will celebrate is...

4

CONCLUSION

Being a CEO brings with it many challenges. How we face those challenges helps to define our success or our failure. Therefore, it is incumbent upon a CEO, and any other leader, to bring the best version of themselves to the table.

Wouldn't you agree?

However, we both know that sometimes bringing our best is easier said than done as it often requires working through some personal challenges first, being honest with ourselves and our behaviors, attitudes and actions. And that can suck! It can also be difficult.

Yet, when you choose to embark on a journey or self-improvement for any reason; wanting to obtain a better role at work, desiring a closer connection in a relation-ship, or simply seeing what is possible in your own selves, you are often beginning a journey into the unknown.

I say 'unknown' because some of what you discover may surprise you, even though you may go on this journey believing you know what you have to unravel.

However, taking the time to uncover your core limiting beliefs, or figuring out what distorted or wounded energy impacts you most, or digging deep into some forgotten memory and releasing its hold on you is a powerful way to show up in your life.

While you may never be the CEO of a company, showing up for yourself consistently, compassionately, and authentically allows you to become the CEO of your life.

Dear Reader,

I wrote this book with the intention of sharing some of my knowledge about leadership. What I realized as I began writing was that the real story was not about actual leadership "stuff", it was about how I got to where I am today, in other words, the journey to leadership.

My journey was, like many people's journeys, not a direct route. It was circuitous, sometimes moving forward, sometimes backwards, and always a little chaotic. There were times that I wanted to give up, times that I questioned my path, and times that I was absolutely certain that this was my purpose in life.

One thing I can say for certain is that once I started down the path of leadership, it was with the vision of being the best leader that I could be.

Now, that vision changed over time…well, maybe it is better to say that my definition of a good leader changed, thus changing how the vision played out in my head thus, I kept my eye on self-improvement.

I imagine that if you are reading this book, you, too, have a vision of being a good leader, or better than you were when you started. And that vision has led to embarking on a journey of self-discovery.

I'd like to invite you to undertake your journey of self-discovery with reverence, compassion, and a wide-eyed sense of adventure. Know that there may be trials and tribulations, but there will also be triumphs and celebrations. Allow space for all of it! It is all valuable, and it is *all* worthy of your time and energy…even the shit-show stuff.

Know that I am holding space for you. You, dear readers, are important to me. You are important to a lot of people. You hold in your hand the power to become the CEO of your life.

Do it!

EnJoy, Life, & Love,

René

René Murata is a visionary leader, CEO, and mentor who's redefining what it means to lead as a woman in today's world. As the founder of CEO Essence and Risk Integrity Safety Knowledge, Inc., René bridges two worlds, the analytical precision of the gas, oil, and petrochemical industries, and the intuitive, heart-centered world of conscious leadership.

After more than two decades thriving in male-dominated environments, René began to see a powerful truth: the very traits women are often told to suppress empathy, intuition, compassion, and emotional intelligence are the ones the world most needs in leadership today. That realization sparked a mission: to help women reclaim their voice, embrace their whole selves, and rise into leadership that is both strong and soulful.

René believes the world is ready for a new paradigm of leadership, one rooted not in dominance or hierarchy, but in humanity, connection, and courage. Her work is dedicated to empowering women to blend the masculine and feminine energies within themselves, transforming the way they lead, live, and love.

Through her coaching, programs, and speaking, René guides conscious women and organizations through the inner work required to lead differently, work that includes self-trust, vulnerability, empathy, and aligned action. She provides practical tools and profound insight to help her clients cultivate confidence, emotional resilience, and authentic presence.

Her philosophy is simple yet revolutionary:

When women lead from alignment rather than exhaustion, when they embody both strength and softness, when they honor their intuition as much as their intellect, they change everything.

René's approach weaves together years of executive experience, certifications in Reiki, breathwork, trauma-informed coaching, and intuitive healing. Her teachings help women shift from control to confidence, from perfection to purpose, and from burnout to balance.

Living what she teaches, René now calls Italy home, where she shares a life rich with laughter, good food, and deep conversation with her husband and children. Whether she's walking cobblestone streets, leading a workshop, or writing her next book, René continues to live her mission: to help women rise, not by becoming someone else, but by coming home to themselves.

Website: ReneMurata.com

Email: Rene.Murata@CEOEssence.com

www.ingramcontent.com/pod-product-compliance
Lightning Source LLC
LaVergne TN
LVHW051813080426
835513LV00017B/1930